THREE TO TANGO

A DANCE OF LOVE, LAUGHTER, AND HOPE

RACHITA BAFNA

This book is dedicated to all those remarkable individuals who have remained unwavering pillars of support throughout my journey, navigating every twist and turn with me. To my dear friends (you know who you are!) who offered their shoulders for my tears, let me unleash my frustrations without judgment, and lent me their patient ears. To my family, despite our diverse perspectives, you extended a safe haven, embraced me and my children with open hearts, and continue to champion our choices without hesitation.

To the individuals who crossed my path, even briefly, your impact has left indelible imprints, imparting life lessons that have sculpted the person I am today.

And lastly, to my incredible children – though I often feel unsure of my parenting, your vitality and happiness are my greatest rewards.

Contents

Contents

Preface

In the intricate tapestry of life, there exist stories that are both deeply personal and universally resonant. This compilation is one such journey—a chronicle of love, resilience, and growth that has unfolded against the backdrop of single motherhood.

Please keep in mind that these blogs are meticulously arranged in the order they were written. This arrangement allows you to walk in my shoes, feeling the balance and sometimes uncertainty that shaped our path to where we stand today.

Through these pages, I invite you into the raw and unfiltered narrative of my parenting voyage. With my two children by my side, we navigated a path unforeseen, carved by the absence of a beloved father. This book is an anthology of the blogs that encapsulate the profound essence of our shared experiences, triumphs, setbacks, and moments of unadulterated joy.

It is a journey that mirrors the unpredictable twists and turns of a rollercoaster ride. In its highs, we reveled in laughter, discovered new strengths, and embraced the profound beauty of our connections. But like any rollercoaster, there were moments of heart-stopping descent, where loss and grief echoed loudly. Yet, we held on, clinging to each other and to the promise of brighter days ahead.

Through these musings, you will join us as we learned to mend our hearts and find our footing once again. It is a testament to the human spirit's remarkable ability to heal and adapt, especially in the face of adversity. Each blog is a page turned in the story of how we forged our identity as a family unit, navigating our shared path with courage and determination.

As you immerse yourself in these pages, you will witness the tapestry of emotions woven into our journey: the tears shed in solitude, the poignant emotions of revisiting the past and the trepidation of stepping into motherhood, the laughter shared around the dinner table, the moments of reflection when the weight of the world seemed too heavy to bear. Through it all, you will glimpse the unwavering bond that has grown between a mother and her children, transcending challenges and turning them into opportunities for growth.

This is an ongoing journey, one without a final destination. As the years unfold, we continue to learn, adapt, and evolve, ever mindful of the precious lessons embedded in every experience. We invite you to walk alongside us, not just as readers, but as fellow travelers, for in our journey, you may find echoes of your own.

May these blogs serve as both a beacon of hope and a mirror reflecting the intricate mosaic of life's myriad shades. Thank you for sharing in our journey of love, loss, laughter, and learning.

CHAPTER ONE

P.S. I Love You

My book can never begin without the mention of my husband. Alok, was not just my husband or the father of my children; he was and always will be the best friend I ever had. I had written this letter to him 10 days after his death. I couldn't process not hearing his voice and not being able to see him. Found this letter today in my old phone, sharing it and hoping that wherever he is...he is happy.

Dear Alok,

Since the time you have gone (been 10 days now) my mind has been blank. I have lost my best friend, my guide, my only boyfriend, the love of my life...I lost YOU!

People want me to be strong for our kids. I am strong. I talk to them, I laugh with them, but my mind stays blank! I'm just a mother now. I miss being your girlfriend, I miss being your wife. When I'm with you, everything makes sense. You make me the person I want to be and not the person I am! Life without you is unbearable!

I've got the whole bed to me, but I don't want it. I don't have anybody snoring next to me, but I miss those snores! I don't want to think about the future because without you, even that is blank! I remember those little tiffs we had over rom-coms and action movies, holding your hand after watching horror flicks and troubling you all night over that! I miss being in your arms...those strong arms that would hold me tight and where I could hide! I only wish I could turn back time.

The kids miss you. They look lost Alok.... it's not easy for them. It's not easy on anyone of us, we all miss you. The kids still shiver at night and they hold me tight, they get scared if they don't see me.

Alok, I know wherever you are, you will be more at peace...but come back please. We just started with the best part of our lives, don't ditch me now. We will get through everything together I promise, just be here with us. Help us

breathe again, help us live again....please just come back, only once come back!
I miss you, come back please.
P.S. I LOVE YOU

CHAPTER TWO

I Am ME!

Lately I've been pretending like everything's okay and that everything around me hasn't collapsed; but this morning I woke up and I realized I was the one who collapsed!

Taking charge of my life has been tough, there have been moments when I have actually wanted to leave everything and run away! There have been days when it looks like a cake walk, I have had people in my life who have seen me and stood by me in all my lows and celebrated all my highs!

To all those people a big **THANKYOU!**

These few months I have learnt a valuable lesson that in the end I need to have peace with myself, I need to stop running after what was and will never be a part of my life again! It's a tough phase but I'll get there!

I have learnt that the people who say they will stay till the end are the ones who leave, so do not depend on anyone but yourself!

I have learnt that instead of getting to know others, I need to know myself! I need to know what makes me laugh, what makes me cry, what makes me angry, what I love! I need to be my best friend again!

I have learnt that my own thoughts are my magic wand and my belief is the magic spell needed to turn my fears into courage. My children are my strength and the only reason to get up and get moving!

I have learnt that I am my own soul-mate, I am a soul and my mate, I STAY!

I have learnt that I am a POEM, I flow in my own rhythm and rhyme, only a few can understand!

I have learnt I am a Dancer and my life is my Dance!

I have learnt that it's my life and I am responsible for making it happy, so no matter what is going on right now, the ending will be a happy one!

CHAPTER THREE

Stop saying Why ME!!!??

Yeah!! Once again proved Life is funny and it definitely doesn't work the way we want it to.....in these few months I have definitely turned wiser and more practical...sometimes I feel I can open my own counselling office!!

Yeah so the most important realisation is that WE work according to how our life wants us to and not the other way around!! We struggle, fight and do all sorts of nonsense just to get our life in order....sometimes we succeed, but other times we end up screwing it up more!!

Naaah!! I'm not a philosopher but yeah practical thinker after all the jolts life gives. Someone has very rightly said that instead of cribbing about what you do not have, just stop, breathe and look around at what you have and learn to appreciate it!! After fighting with God and my own life to get it on track for months I finally gave up!! Yup! Gave up! Instead of fighting I decided to just go with the flow...I sat down and looked around, I saw my kids and I smiled genuinely in ages!

I decided to stop fighting and give myself another chance at starting life afresh, like a new beginning and though it sounds cliché, but instead of saying WHY ME? I said TRY ME!! I know I'm a Gladiator, I will survive, but I also know it would take time for life to be as it was and trust me I'm okay with everything as long as my kids are happy...they are the strength that keeps me going on and keeps me strong!

Like every cloud has a silver lining I'm sure mine does too and I'm just waiting to see it because even if faintly I know I'm going to go grab it with both hands and never let it go!!

CHAPTER FOUR

My MOM...hats off to you!

Why do kids have to grow up!?

As a kid I always wanted to grow up fast...in school.... I wanted college and in college wanted to work!

After growing up I understood... growing up is not easy, all those years of pestering my mother just flew by.

She would tell me "slow down", but I would just want to do everything quickly.

When she would be really angry she would shout "the day you have kids of your own, I'll see how you handle them!" Or she would tell me "when you have kids of your own you will understand!"

I used to laugh it all away thinking that I will never marry...never did I know that not only would I be in a hurry to marry, but I would be in a hurry to have kids too. After having kids and handling them along with my 3rd overgrown kid (my darling husband) and the household work too...have I realised that my mother used to do more than what I have done so far...she used to work and still take out time to stitch us frocks & soft toys, knit sweaters for us and read us stories at night!!

I feel soo bad that never did I even once tell her that Mumma I LOVE YOU and yes you will always be my inspiration! Thank you sooo much for everything you have done with us and for us. We are what we are because of you and are very proud that YOU are our mother!

Years have gone by and now I know that I'm walking in your footsteps, I am becoming a more independent and strong woman...just like you! When I'm stuck somewhere I think of how you would solve it and nothing seems impossible.

Now I want to slow down with you...let you relive all the moments again with your grandchildren with no worries of the studies part...you can spoil your grandchildren rotten...you do not need to worry because I know that we grew up to be good humans, so our kids will too have your teachings instilled in them.

I wish to be a mother to my kids just as you are with us and pray that they are just as proud of me as we are of you!

I LOVE YOU HANNA!!!!! No one could be a better mom

CHAPTER FIVE

I Choose To Live

"*You Chose*
You chose.
You chose.
You chose.
You chose to give away your love.
You chose to have a broken heart.
You chose to give up.
You chose to hang on. You chose to react.
You chose to feel insecure.
You chose to feel anger.
You chose to fight back.
You chose to have hope. You chose to be naïve.
You chose to ignore your intuition.
You chose to ignore the advice.
You chose to look the other way.
You chose to not listen.
You chose to be stuck in the past. You chose your perspective.
You chose to blame.
You chose to be right.
You chose your pride.
You chose your games.
You chose your ego.
You chose your paranoia.
You chose to compete.
You chose your enemies.
You chose your consequences. You chose.
You chose.

You chose.

You chose.

However, you are not alone. Generations of women in your family have chosen. Women around the world have chosen. We all have chosen at one time in our lives. We stand behind you now screaming:

Choose to let go.

Choose dignity.

Choose to forgive yourself.

Choose to forgive others.

Choose to see your value.

Choose to show the world you're not a victim.

Choose to make us proud."

— *Shannon L. Alder* "

I came across this poem by Shannon L Alder and just loved it....we choose things that shape up our life.

I chose to marry a wonderful man who gave me the best gift ever...my two beautiful children. Starting a new life with my children is still not a cakewalk, but we are trying, little baby steps at a time. They look at me for strength while I look at them because they are my strength. Our loved ones can help us, but ultimately it is the three of us who need to live our own life, nobody can do it for us. I realize that we are not Victims of fate, rather we are survivors and we only know how to move on...

Life is beautiful, every day is a new beginning and we should keep it that way. My 35-year life has taught me that life is too short and precious to hold grudges or anger...let it go! LIVE in the present, our choices shaped our life to what it is today so stop complaining and do something about it! Every day you wake up, thank God to give you another day to make new choices, hold on to those choices whether bad or good, because bad choices have given us lessons to be learned and good choices have given us opportunities to move forward.

I have chosen to not sit and cry, rather move ahead and LOVE... love life, love the flowers, the colours, the wind messing my hair, the little arguments with my children over clothes and food, the bedtime stories and goodnight hugs, giggles and kisses...THIS is life and this is what I choose.

As I sit wondering what this new year has to offer me and my kids, I realized it is I who needs to show the world what I can do, because it is not the year that matters...

Ultimately it is what I can do to make this year different from the last one. As long as we are breathing, it is a new beginning every day. With a whole new life ahead of us, we have to be strong enough to face all the challenges that come our way and win! Yes WIN, Succeed!! I have met people who tell me this is a new chapter in my life...I do not agree, this is a whole new book...a book that will be written by me and my children, we have to ensure it is written beautifully and with LOVE!

CHAPTER SIX

Who are you?

Have you ever had that feeling or realisation that you are not the person you try to be, that you are a totally different person in reality but are pretending to be someone you are not, only to fit into your surroundings!!?That feeling when you feel you are caged???

All your life you want to be like everybody you love, you try and subdue your real self to be the person that everyone loves!! But in trying to keep everybody happy you end up punishing yourself! Then one day you get up with the realisation that the person you see in the mirror is not you! The Real you is forced to sit in a corner, just with a gleam hope of being let out someday!

The real you pleads to come out many times and you end up ignoring all the pleads, since you feel that the people around you might not like it. But my question is that how can you love others if you do not love yourself???

Why do we need to try and fit in with people, why are we afraid to show our real selves? I say it with experience...we can be Happy just being our own self. I used to be the same, I would be one person with my friends and a totally different person in front of someone else....adapt myself or change my behaviour, my likes and dislikes according to the people surrounding me. In the end when it became too much and I couldn't recognize my own self, I broke down...I was scared that people will not like me for just being me...but I was wrong! Now I live life on my terms and there are people who like me for the REAL ME!

I know it is not easy, but it is not tough too. Take yourself out on a date, learn what are YOUR likes and dislikes. Travel alone, dress up take out some 'Me time', do what makes you happy...if you are happy then the people around you will be happy. Always remember you are your own best friend and nobody can know you better.

So love yourself and please be YOU.....the REAL you whom you also love!

If you love yourself others would also love you!!! So ask yourself just one question...WHO are YOU???

The Art of Whistling

For almost 20 years of my life I have been mesmerized by different kinds of whistles.....yes you read it right WHISTLES! It is a talent all by itself...to my Mom who I know is reading this... I'm sorry (to her).....I know you would get mad reading this!

So the back story is like the way most of the girls born in the 80's was brought up....with strict instructions to not whistle. I was brought up with my mom always telling me and my sister to not whistle as it is a bad habit and with the superstitious belief of some bad luck attacking people who whistle.

But that is not what I'm writing about....I learnt the normal whistle in school...the simple one. My obsession..yes the OBSESSION with whistling didn't end there...I wanted to learn how to whistle with fingers in the mouth...the one that is really loud and shrill..the typical Desi style of whistle. I used to always ask my husband to teach me finger whistle since he was a pro at that! Alas! That couldn't happen. Being a single mom for 4 years, my kids and I have become more like friends and trust me we still are doing lots of "firsts" together. So, recently the three of us were watching a YouTube video about whistling and trying our luck at it. To my surprise in just four tries my son learnt the finger whistle.

I must confess at first jealous, later I was proud of how quick he learnt something I was still struggling with, and then I did feel a little guilty for his learning the art of whistling. But hey! How else would he learn all this! So we have a new ritual every Sunday where he teaches me how to finger whistle and I fail miserably, to the extent of sometimes being covered in saliva. Nonetheless, he still keeps his patience, a small umbrella and a napkin besides him and religiously makes it a point to try and teach me again every Sunday...hopefully I will someday learn this art of whistling! Wish me luck!

CHAPTER EIGHT

My confusingly sweet experience!

There's something inside me....something growing in me, the doctor calls it a BABY....

I'm supposed to be very excited and I am with the news of being pregnant....but why can I not connect with it??? I was scared and had nightmares about the way my life would change. I was about to be responsible for another tiny human...HUMAN...the word would send shivers down my spine, it felt more like an alien in my body. Months go by and as my bump grows I feel something moving in me.

There was a time when the idea of something inside me would freak me out but now I'm in love with this feeling...slowly 'it' becomes a part of me. Nights on end as my bump grows bigger and it gets more difficult to sleep, rather than being upset or irritated...I'm loving it!

This 'thing' inside me makes me eat almost any time of the day or night, it seems it likes junk food more than healthy food, loves green apple more than the red ones....my clothes get tighter and I'm fitting in my husband's clothes (he's healthier than I am ;) sorry!!!) for a girl (of 23yrs old) clothes getting tighter should've made me angry but I was in love with the feeling. Morning sickness made it impossible for me to eat anything but cakes and ice-creams, then started the tantrums of drinking apple juice, specifically green apples' juice and freshly made. This 'thing' has a sweet tooth and loves juice at 3:00AM, loves pani puri for breakfast and there goes my weight, skyrocketing to 80kgs from what was 40, I should be angry but I'm not! Then the 'D' day came....I was very excited and scared at the same time...I only remember doctors and nurses around me and their equipment!

After a few hours of sleep (that's what it was for me!), I felt a small tiny hand punching my face, as I opened my eyes....there HE was....MY

BABY!...YES BABY! He was not SOMETHING....he was a PART of Me and lying down quietly next to me like he knew I'm the mother and I picked him up with ease as if I was born a professional at handling babies. All my doubts, all my fears suddenly go away somehow and I was filled with joy.

We connected instantly...the most beautiful experience of my life!

CHAPTER NINE

MOM

13 years ago, full of dreams, with a penchant for drama, a 22 year old girl got an opportunity. An opportunity which she willingly got ready to explore with the love of her life.

Fainting a few times through the nervousness and excitement of the process, she made her way through the labyrinth of everything that has to do with motherhood

The realisation doesn't really hit till the time the first cry of the baby calms down with your touch, your mere presence That I am a MOM Read it back to front or front to back I am a MOM Try reading it upside down, WOW I am a MOM I always desired for Sleepless nights, partying, chilling with friends till the night was exhausted Here, Instead I was feeling the chill with my first born The usual clink of revelry was replaced with the care of milk bottles, and steps on the dance floor were replaced with cleaning an innocent mess on the floor Countless late night feeds, endless nappy changes was my routine

Bear in mind, I would still run to my mum whenever I had risen temperature. I was still THAT girl

But now, I was handling it for my new born after every single vaccination shot & more. After Trial and error, hit and miss, analysis, observation, experiments...I was the Dexter of my laboratory. Sundays that were filled with brunches, and my munchkin.

And almost as if this experience was not enough, I had another opportunity knocking soon - my daughter! As they say, one is lucky to get the opportunities. But it's the hard work that you put into those opportunities which make them a reason for your Smile :) I am still THAT girl But I know, I am also much, much more!

CHAPTER TEN

What would I do for you!

"I would do just about anything you'd ask,
For you there's nothing I wouldn't do, there's no such task. I would walk without my shoes to the end of the Earth,
I would give up anything I had to, to teach you self-worth. I would hold your hand every minute of every day,
But I won't because I know you need to find your own way. I would surely bear the heartache of your first love that's real,
Even though I can't, I will naturally feel as you feel. I would sell my soul if it would keep you happy forever,
I would give my right arm to keep us forever together. I would run a hundred miles up-hill in the rain,
Just to guarantee that you will never feel pain. I would laugh with you even if I was sad,
I will give you a smile even if I'm mad. I can only accept your mistakes with a grin on my face,
I will guide you in correcting them, but at your own pace. I will guide you through life, as this world can get quite wild,
Just don't you ever forget that you will always be my child.
-Jayne Sena"

Surfing the net I came across this poem by Jayne Sena, I could so relate to it.... Naman and Dimple when you do read this.....I would really want you to know that I am Sorry....I know I'm not the PERFECT MOM and I scold both of you, but know this I love you with all my life and nothing can ever lessen my love for the two of you. Yes I agree our life has changed drastically, but know this....the three of us are doing real good and we will swim through it all with our heads held high! I can't wait for the two of you to grow up and share with me all the things that happen in your life, just the way you do now every day. Always remember, there is nothing I wouldn't do for the two of you but babies the world is a very tricky place, be nice to people but do not let them use your niceness to their advantage and your loss. I am here always for any advice and any talk....I'm here as your mother, father and your friend! Your first crush, your first heartbreak, your first everything....we are in it together and we will always correct each other when either one of us are wrong! I love it when you trouble me, tease me like I'm younger to you two and when it's my birthday...you two surprise me by acting so mature!! We are a weird crazy set of three and that madness in the three of us will never die, we were born to be wild and crazy which we are and will continue to be....so no matter what happens in life, keep this craziness alive, trust me when I say this it gets one out with ease through the unimaginable!! When you grow up and start a life of your own...remember for me you will still be the little babies I held in my hands years ago, I will still correct you if you go wrong, I will still fight with you, I will still tease you but most of all....I will still Love You!!! Always be the sweet, wild, crazy set of kids you are.....your father will always be proud of you!!

CHAPTER ELEVEN

An Ode to 2019

"Here's to the ones that we got,
Cheers to the wish you were here, but you're not
'Cause the drinks bring back all the memories
Of everything we've been through
Toast to the ones here today
Toast to the ones that we lost on the way
'Cause the drinks bring back all the memories
And the memories bring back, memories bring back you.
- Maroon 5"

A friend, philosopher, a guide is what 2019 has been for me, but most importantly it has been a teacher. As I look back at the year gone by, I can't help but hum this song by Maroon 5. This song hits the right chords and maybe a lot more people like me can relate with it.

2019 has taught me to be grateful for everything and everyone I have in my life. I know I have grown more this year than the last. All the trials and errors have just made me wiser. My kids have been my biggest strength and this year our bond has grown stronger, strong enough to not let anyone disrupt it. To all the people that I have met or spoken with...Thank you

2019 has taught me to be stronger but have my occasional break downs and not feel guilty about it. It has taught me not to beg people to stay, but to move on gracefully. 2019 has taught me to be a role model for my kids and teach them to be independent. It has taught me to not be afraid to cut off people or things that pull me down, to not be afraid to chase my dreams.

I know I have an amazing family and friends who will do anything for me at the drop of a hat, I have learnt to cherish them and never hurt them. But the most important thing that 2019 has taught me is to make myself a priority, to do things that make me happy, and not feel guilty about it. After all a happy me can help me make my people happy. To not be afraid to love and never lose my smile.

2019 Thank you for everything that you have taught me and making me a more confident woman.

2020 gear up, because I'm a whole new me and I'm coming for you!

Somewhere over the Rainbow

""Somewhere over the rainbow, way up high
There' s a land that I heard of once in a lullaby,
Somewhere over the rainbow, skies are blue,
And the dreams that you dare to dream, really do come true...""

This song by Judy Garland, can still mesmerise a person and take one to a whole new place.

So, I am a mom to a preteen and a teenager...it does get really messy at times and I wonder why can't kids just be kids or directly grow into adults? Why does this phase of preteens and teens have to be there?

Earlier the kids would go to school, tuitions and games so there would be ample time for me to do MY things, have ME TIME and not have to worry too much. Thanks to COVID and the lockdown, three months in the house with no friends and no help was a real eye opener.

Basically, I am not the problem...I blame my sun sign, so the problem is with my sun sign...Pisces! You see Pisceans are known to have a bad reputation of being known as the "over thinkers!"

This bout of Overthinking got me one fine day, so here is how it goes....three months of the lockdown I was absolutely fine, the kids and I managed ourselves perfectly well. Of late I started losing my temper, would cry for no reason, I started feeling like I'm stuck, suffocated, became more quiet, and to top it all fought with a dear friend for no reason whatsoever. This friend of mine told me I'm overthinking things that are not even there!

Now you need to understand that 36 years of my life, nobody has ever told me that I "Overthink!" Well, this was the eye opener....this lockdown was getting to me, my loneliness was getting to me....I had started harming myself.

This lockdown taught me many things but the worse was it pushed me into overanalysing stuff and unknowingly I was doing it, it was the cause of the change in my behaviour! It's been 5 years that I've been living on my own with my kids, we have faced all our struggles together and have become stronger with each challenge. But this was my fight with myself and I couldn't fail.

So, I sat down and spoke with myself....you see the worst part of overthinking or overanalysing things is that one cannot sleep properly at night, because, well, the brain is working constantly. This is what was happening with me, I was not sleeping well, not sleeping for more than 3 hours at night.

I was chanting everyday but it somehow became tougher by the day, I used to wonder if my kids would be better off without me....I had to take control of myself or else I would lose everything and everyone dear to me. It was not easy controlling your thoughts but I was adamant and one day I finally took a pad and wrote the names of everyone and everything that make me happy, people whose thought gets a smile on my face, my kids who give me a reason to wake up and a sense of purpose in life, my family and friends who love me.

I realised that thinking about what will happen in the future or how it will happen is not going to get me anywhere and in turn will simply spoil my present. I am grateful for all the people in my life because they have all been there for a reason and have taught me something valuable in their own ways. This has been a journey for me and I have learnt that even though my life is still messy, it's not perfect and I'm learning things everyday but it is my life and I have control on it. Whether the choices I make are right or wrong, they are my choices and hey! Wrong choices only keep us strayed from our purpose for a while but it somehow gets us back to making the right choices and closer to our goals.

It feels good to write about it and yes this is what the song has done for me, I've crossed the rainbow into a land that has all my favourite people and even though I can't physically meet them right now, I know they are always by my side and love me no matter what. They are all I need, also not to forget, COFFEE and I'm happy!

17 Again

I am a single mother to two teenagers, a boy and a girl with only a year's gap and this is my story.

Lately, I've been reading all these posts on how parents should handle their kids and trust me it's scary. Every time I read these articles, I get scared because they make me feel like having kids is scary and they should be treated like a project. Well, my experience so far has just made me realize, that yes raising kids is not an easy task, but it is not impossible.

When my son was born, initially I was lost, didn't know if I could handle being a mom, but thanks to my mother-in-law, I gained the confidence I needed. She taught me that everybody's way of raising their kids is different, you just need to figure out what way suits you and that happens only by trial and error. You try something, if it works...very good and if it doesn't, see what went wrong and correct it.

The entire phase of my kids being my babies to my kids being my friends has been amazing. Well, truth be told...this transition gave me a lot of hair fall!! I was so used to doing everything for them, all the times they needed me and they depended on me...I guess I missed it.

My kids entering their teens has been harder on me, my entire life revolved around them. I always had them as an excuse to avoid plans with my friends, they would need help with their studies, projects and homework, and they would want me in the house always and hold me and sleep at night. They would hug me every day, fight to sit on my lap, tell me to decide their clothes and all this made me feel USEFUL, WANTED and IMPORTANT. I felt like even if nothing went right in my life...I would still have one important job and that is being their mom.

The transition starts when the kids are pre-teens....the age group of 11-12 years is the most confusing, they say something and it means something else. For me, handling not 1 but 2 kids in this phase was really challenging, I would spend time with them, but they would want their "space", the lunches with chitter-chatter changed to rushed-up lunch. My daughter had her "Goth" phase but minus the black nail polish. At times it felt like I had two sons...I was picking up same colour and size shorts and t-shirts from the "boys" section in twos. Black was the new trend in my house! The worst was when she turned 11, a month before her birthday, we were deciding on the theme and I wanted to buy her a dress and she wanted shorts...this argument(yes an argument, because apparently she was all of a sudden a grown up and wanted to be heard!) went on for almost a week, till I threatened to cancel the party altogether. Finally we made a deal where I would buy my daughter a nice girly dress for her birthday, which she would wear till the cake is cut and pictures taken, theme was her choice, food was mine and yes the most important....the cake was BLACK!

My son on the other hand wasn't like this, no demands...so thank god! But, he would take offence to anything and everything I would say...things like "brush your teeth", "take a shower" were sentences that were the most offensive...he would literally only say one thing..."Mom, you mean I don't brush and shower every day or do you mean I have a memory issue that you need to remind me of these things daily!" 'Rebel' is the right word, asking him to change his clothes to go out meant he would just change his t-shirt. Shirts were his enemy, hoodies his friend...in the peak of summer he would be dressed in a hoodie and shorts. All this new lingo he was speaking in, made me feel old and obsolete, but like everything else I'm glad this phase passed too and I survived it! I would be lying if I said I wasn't scared. In fact, I questioned my ability to be a mom, I would feel like I didn't know my kids anymore and would cry myself to sleep.

Dealing with my kids as pre-teens, I learnt that meeting them in between is not so bad...it's just a temporary phase and eventually passes. The kids in this age are themselves confused about what they like and what they dislike, so instead of forcing our ideology on them, once in a while its okay to compromise on a few things. Just like with drinks, mixing them makes a whole new fun drink, a cocktail....that's what is needed in this phase (quite literally for moms to unwind sometimes!), mix their ideas with our own and you never know, what a fun new idea develops.

Enter teens, I still don't get what these guys do...but all I know is they are more than siblings, they are each other's confidants, best friends, chums, partners in crime etc. Where do I fit in it all? I'm the third musketeer, yes I am, and together we are the three musketeers. I'm still their mother, but more than that, I've somehow transitioned into a friend for them. I no longer feel lonely, I have accepted the fact that they are growing up and soon they will have to leave the nest in order to fly and soar high! We watch things on the television and if in don't understand, I ask now and they, very patiently explain. When I'm unwell they look after me, just the way I do for them. They finish their homework on their own and are more serious about their studies but at the same time, I ensure they have some play in between all the work. Somewhere, I suppose the lockdown played a vital role for our bonding to grow stronger, since there were no maids, we distributed all the household chores and shared all the responsibilities and duties. Sometimes, I get confused who is raising whom? Who is the parent and who are the kids? There are times I'm teaching them things and then there are moments where they are the teacher and I, the student. I'm enjoying this teenage with them, we are more open with each other, we talk and share everything that is happening in our lives and there isn't anything that they wouldn't know about me just as I know everything about them. When they are a little difficult to handle, instead of shouting or scolding, I talk it out with them, ask them to put themselves in that situation and tell me how would they react or feel.

Their teenage is teaching me that no matter how young or old kids are, they always need their mother, we just need to be there as a friend, philosopher and guide subjected to the situation or circumstances at that moment. Also, just go with the flow, enjoy these little moments because once the kids are out for college or work, we will only have these memories to cherish!

I can't wait for them to actually be adults and all the new experiences that await me. My kids are my world and will always be, and no matter where they are I will love them forever.

CHAPTER FOURTEEN

Blunder to Wonder of Motherhood

"Motherhood" the word is enough to make anyone fret and worry, I agree because I still remember how scared I was when I got the news of being pregnant. My motherhood journey so far has been full of ups and downs, it's like a movie...action, drama (LOADS OF IT!), emotions, dance, romance believe me when I say this, everything but songs has been there in my journey.

I was just 23 years old when my son was born, naïve as ever, for me he was just another doll.....till he started pooping and crying! That's when I realised I was a MOTHER, I was responsible for cleaning him and taking care of this little human. I couldn't just play with him and give him away when he cried, I had to wake up at night and feed him, I felt like a cow, always pumping milk and when I wasn't busy pumping...I was leaking milk! Not that he was breastfeeding, but nonetheless I was pumping, why? Because I read books on motherhood and to be a "good mother" I wanted him to have my milk! I was glad when I stopped producing milk, not that it mattered because 10 days into motherhood, I realised those books on motherhood were useless for me, I had to rely on what I want to eat so that the baby likes it too and BAMMM.. day 10 I fed my baby a few drops of pani puri and he loved it!

The trials and errors of my first baby were not over, I was still having my learning experiences with him and I got the news that I was pregnant AGAIN!!! So handling this guy with a baby in me was not that great but thankfully I had that support system to manage it comfortably till I delivered my DAUGHTER! I was barely out of diapers and bottles and now again I was into it. Most of the nights I cried because I had had enough with all the responsibilities. There were times when I would be feeding my son rice and would end up putting it in my daughter's mouth (who was just a new-born), and again put my finger in her mouth to take it out. Basically, I was a walking zombie who smelled only of poop, vomits and rash creams...gone were the days of dressing up and feeling good (or so I thought!)

So basically the initial 7-10 years were all about kids, the same worries and complains like any other mother on this planet. Now that they are teenagers, it's more relaxed I still worry about their studies and future, but I know, that as a family, all of us will ensure they do well because we are working together for the kids' bright future. I am enjoying their teenage phase, they are my kids and I bring out my "khadoos mother" instincts sometimes when I feel they are crossing the line; but mostly I'm the "embarrassing mother" who loves embarrassing them whenever I get the chance.

There are times when they are on a video call and I wouldn't know who is on the call, but I would barge in dancing or singing or shouting....anything to embarrass them! Their friends call me the "cool mom" but really I cannot take the credit entirely...I am a cool mom of two rather cool kids. I know we are what we are because of each other. Now I even have time to myself and sometimes a little too much for my liking, we joke about boyfriends and girlfriends and whenever I tell them I have a "date" they know it is with myself and the only "affair" I have is with COFFEE, because coffee is life! But on a serious note...once in a week three of us go on a date with each other.

The best bit about them growing up is that now I can dress up, go out, celebrate, smell amazing, look sexy, learn new dance forms and teach them...because I need good dance partners, live healthily and party with them.

In my house, I am the only drama queen, we make our own rules, then we break some, then we make our own traditions...then we break some....but the bottom line is that we are growing up together, I have a lot of my "firsts" with my kids....again, that's a whole new blog! I'm still on my ride of this scary yet fun rollercoaster ride called Motherhood and my advice to all the mothers out there.....enjoy it while it lasts but don't forget yourself in the process.

CHAPTER FIFTEEN

Confessions of a spent-out mom!

There is a famous quote by Jill Churchill, *"There's no way to be a perfect mother and a million ways to be a good one."*

Why am I starting my blog with this quote? That's for the simple reason that yes I'm not a perfect mother...I'm far away from being perfect, but with all my imperfections I know that I am a good mother. Being single and handling all the roles that I play every single day of my life I get exhausted and frankly speaking, bored!

But I guess that's what happens when you are a mother and most of the days only a mother. So how do I keep my sanity? Well, that's a secret...which I know will no longer be one when I tell you all, but what the hell! So basically, I've been a mother for almost 14 years now (My son turns 14 in a few months!) since it's me handling their tantrums most of the time, it's kind of gets to me...I start losing my cool and sometimes I just wish I could forward the entire time to them being settled with their work so that I could be free from these tantrums and basically being on my toes always.

Months go by before I get time to myself, even if they are visiting relatives, I can't because I have to work! When they aren't around there are other things that need my attention whether in the house or work. So basically, I'm just working all the time. Just when this started affecting my health I realised that I haven't lived for myself, haven't done things I want to do and haven't eaten things I like....everything in my house has always been around the kids and their likes and dislikes.

Thanks to the Covid situation, I have been stuck in the house but pre-covid times I would tell the kids that I have some work and just go out with my friends for coffee or for dinner and the kids would be home. I remember when we were visiting my parents, I left the kids there saying I'm visiting a friend and ended up taking a solo vacation (even though it was over a weekend) to Goa. I did tell them after I came back, but I guess we all as mothers need a vacation with no work and nobody to hover around us.

Even now, when they are visiting their grandparents, I also take a mini vacation which I tell them about and they do understand, but I do it, why do I do it? So that I don't get frustrated and be a good mom. It's not that I don't love my kids but I don't want to sacrifice my mental and physical health for them. If I have duties towards my kids, I have a duty towards myself too!

I love being a mother but I don't want the real me to die too...I want to live happy so I can keep my kids happy!

CHAPTER SIXTEEN

How Do You Handle the loss of a Loved One?

How do you handle the loss of a loved one? My life has been nothing short of a movie, I lost my dad at a very young age of 8 years, it was tough but my mother is a strong lady and I have always admired the way she brought up me and my sister. She had the help of her parents and siblings and that's why we are the close-knit family that we are. I still remember that I never spoke to her about my father's accident and now I realize if I had, it would have been easier to talk on this topic. While studying in college I met my husband, believe it or not I met him in my sister's wedding, knew him for only 4 days and decided I wanted to marry him.

We had a lovely ride or a married life till it lasted, sad enough I lost him in a very freakishly similar accident like my father's and my son was my age...8 years! It hasn't been easy for me to be a single mother but yes I learnt a lot from my mother and the mistakes I made that have made me a strong woman.

The most difficult part that has been for me is to get both my kids to deal with the fact that their father is no more and will never come back, initially they used to cry about it, which made me sad and feel helpless, but somehow I was okay with it because they didn't bottle up their feelings. My daughter was easy to handle and explain things, but my son unknowingly started bottling up his feelings. He would take offence to every single small thing that was said to him. He was starting to become a bully too, luckily our family realized it soon enough and we all handled him together.

But then again, it is tough for a kid to come to terms with such a huge loss. I remember, he had an essay writing class in school, and his class teacher sent me a picture of the essay he wrote. She called me and told me that she had tears in her eyes while reading his essay, he had written about the time he spent with his dad and how he misses him. That day I realized he needed to vent out all his feelings, it was tough for me to keep a strong face and hold back my tears, because I missed my husband, but somebody had to talk to my son and that somebody had to be me. I sat down with him and spoke about the whole accident, I made him comfortable to talk to me about his feelings.

We would go out for ice-creams, milkshakes and I would ask him about his favourite memories with his dad. I told him that he doesn't need to grow up so soon, that we are all there to look after him, I wasn't going to let him repeat the same mistake I made of not speaking about how he felt. Both the kids know that they have nothing to fear and that they are not inferior to anyone, I also made them realize that they have many people who love them dearly and though they don't have a father, they are surrounded by people who will do anything for them at the drop of a hat!

It's been 5 years and we are all proud of the way they are growing up and the way they handle themselves. Yes they are more independent and yes they have matured more that the kids their age, but they know we are all here for them now and forever!

CHAPTER SEVENTEEN

My Firsts

We often talk and celebrate our child's "firsts"...his/her first word, first step, first smile so on and so forth. We take pictures or reminders, anything to keep that memory fresh and memorable always. But have you ever thought about your own 'firsts?' We as women tend to forget to celebrate our own milestones or experiences. Do you remember the first time you learnt something new, like anything even a small thing like cooking...when was the first time you cooked something and how many attempts did you make to perfect it?

I have had a lot of memorable firsts, when I got married, the first dish I cooked was 'bhindi (okra)', only because I didn't want to admit it, but, that was the only vegetable I knew how to cook...surprisingly it came out tasty. There was a time when we had guests over and I was asked to make pav-bhaji, scared I followed all the instructions on the box of the pav-bhaji masala and it turned out just fine.

There are a lot of firsts as a mom, but again they are my firsts as a 'mother', not 'me.' There was this time when I was taking a solo-trip when I booked plane tickets for myself for the first time and I was really proud of myself, turns out what I booked was the wrong route but I did it and I did it with nobody's help.

The first time I changed a bulb, for many people it may not be a big deal, but when my kids and I started living independently, I was responsible for the house and electricals, scared but I learnt it...I learnt how to change a bulb, I learnt how to fill water in the inverter battery, I learnt how to pay the electricity bill. Trust me standing in the line to pay it was the worse, I went around asking people where to go and which window do I look for paying the bill. There were people who laughed at me for not knowing the basic stuff, but I didn't let that pull me down...finally the person whom I paid the bill to, told me I could pay online and showed me how to do it. Till date

I'm thankful to him, I don't need to stand in the long, tiring line and I am grateful for it.

It is not that I am not scared, I have so many responsibilities that there are times I feel helpless or like running away, but then I have these amazing kids who help me celebrate every new thing I learn, in other words, they celebrate my 'firsts.'

I still do not know many things and I will have many more firsts, but that we will just have to wait and watch. All I know is that I am teaching my kids all this too, so that they never feel lost like I did. Whoever reads this, please do share your firsts, let us all celebrate it together!

CHAPTER EIGHTEEN

The Downside of Online Classes

This is one topic I was avoiding to talk about, everyone has their own opinions. But today while having breakfast, which we do during the breaks between classes, my daughter told me about this incident that happened with a few of her classmates.

Since the schools have been online, many parents have been feeling the pressure and so do the teachers. I have full respect for the teachers and I know they work really hard to impart knowledge to our kids and I'm sure their work pressure has increased more since the online classes have begun, but this incident was appalling. My daughter told me that her teacher during the Zoom class, called out the names of a few children whose fee wasn't paid, a few of them said they will ask their parents and a few said they have paid, but without a second thought she removed them from. The class and put them in the waiting room.

Why do we do this? Why were the kids asked about it....the is a nice and decent way to say this, it could have been reframed as, "remind your parents to pay the fees." Why do the teachers not understand how humiliating and embarrassing it is for the kids? Such careless actions leave an everlasting impact on the mental health of children and they are not that matured to take care of finances or to keep track of their "school fee." I may not be that child's mother, but I am a Mother and I can feel how insulting it is and how hurtful it can be for a child.

I agree the school fees has to be paid and the teachers are also simple following instructions, but something needs to be changed, our system should be changed. The perspective needs to be changed, online classes are no that helpful, but it is a satisfaction that the kids are not wasting their time doing nothing. But again, they are slaves of the screen.

Apart from this incident, personally, these online classes are more of a pain, since both my children are at home the whole day and to top it all, every break in between classes, they want something to eat. When I ask them what they would like to eat they simply say...."give us options!" sometimes I feel these online classes should be for mothers, to learn how to handle themselves with such monsters in the house. Monsters, yes because they make me work!

They always ask for the things that have either finished or they had just a couple of days back...they will never eat what is available in the house. I'm sure they don't have to exercise or lift weights in their classes, but they sure do behave like they are the ones who are tired. They will come out of the rooms and lie down on the couch complaining about how their legs are paining or hands are paining....seriously!? When I ask them to come out for a walk, they have all the excuses in the world and during their classes, even if I tell them that I'm going to buy vegetables, they will be ready to come with me, for the simple reason that I'll feel lonely. God!

The other day, they wanted to eat macaroni for breakfast but they asked me to follow my mother's recipe, I did just that...made it exactly the same way and tasted the same too. My kids....just ate one bite and rejected it all together saying it didn't taste like my mom's macaroni. Then there is this other incident when my son asked me what can I make for snack time and I gave him options...this bugger tells me that his friend's mother makes some amazing dishes for his friend to eat and started showing me the pictures that his friend shared, with a cheeky smile he was like, "Mom why don't you make something like this? Nahi, toh recipe le lo unse!" I was so mad, I told him, "next time when you are hungry go to your friend's mother, don't ask me to cook!" YES my kids are MONSTERS!

I just pray this COVID situation improves, if not for any other reason but at least to save more mothers like me from their brats!

CHAPTER NINETEEN

Live your Life!

Opinions are important, but it's not important to always follow these opinions.

Though twisting and tweaking, these opinions offer the best solution to your need.

After going through one of the Facebook statuses and the posts in general on social media, I wondered about the impact of these opinions.

Instead of learning the hard way it is better to do things that would make us happy, opinions are formed no matter what we do. No matter how good you are if someone wants to judge you, they will and nothing you do will change their opinion. So, stop whining....the best way to live life is the way we wish to!

Don't wait to just celebrate birthdays and anniversaries but celebrate YOURSELF, EACH DAY, EACH MOMENT.

Every day is a reason to celebrate, the women who have their husbands busy with work, don't fret it....just take one off with your girlfriends or your kids or better still just take yourself and go out!! You deserve it!

A very sweet person once told me if you are bothered over something, just dress up, put on your shoes and go get your hair cut!! Try it, it is indeed a mood elevator. If you don't want to cut your hair, go and colour them, highlight them get some bold colours that would bring out the real you and make that 'Badass' statement!

Many a time, we bother too much about others opinions about us, that we start living our lives according to those people. Most of our lives are spent trying to keep everyone around us happy, that we forget our likes and wishes. It is these 'Uncustomized opinions' of others that intervene in our personal space and ultimately creep into our relations.

Entire life we just try to 'Fit' into other's perceived opinions but how can one fit into what is not for them? Read it again!

Better is to look crisp and clean in being You than being a MissFit.

CHAPTER TWENTY

Who Is The Kid Here?

Living with my kids for almost 14 years has been nothing short of a roller coaster ride! Alright, you got me, I confess that I have used this line in most of my blogs....but its true!! I have learnt, a lot thanks to my children, right from being a mother, to being a good human. I thank them for keeping me grounded.

Sometimes when I post a picture on Instagram of my kids and me, I usually use the #(hashtag) 'whoisthekidhere'. Earlier it used to be just to make myself feel younger, but as I grow older, I have realised we do become wiser but we remain kids always.

Okay, maybe I am blabbering here but lately when I actually think about it, there are many things we learn from our kids. People who know me, definitely know my journey so far as a mother. So lately, I've learnt this from my kids...it is true that our children need us, but more than them, it is us as parents who need them. Basically, when they are with me, I hardly get time to sit and ponder, but recently when they were visiting their grand-parents, that's when I realized how much I am dependent on them. This thought scared me, yes you read it right...I am scared because I am dependent on my kids and not physically or financially...but emotionally! This is something that kind of disturbed me. Now I know that for the last 14 years we have never been apart for a long time and I brag to my friends in a very cool manner that, I don't miss them when they are not with me or that it's a normal thing, but the fact is...I MISS THEM!

Why am I scared? The answer is very simple, I want them to succeed in life; just like every parent wants for their children. But the thing is, if they know how dependent I am on them emotionally, when they get good opportunities, I get scared they might start giving up on them to keep me comfortable. I feel somewhere I might just become that chain or that albatross around their neck and they wouldn't be able to fly and reach new highs in life. It may sound stupid, but yeah that's what I have realized and learnt from them. They are my children and they love me, but I don't want me to become their weakness or a responsibility ever!

The other thing that my children taught me is to do things I want to do, they made me realise that while I taught them to make themselves a priority, and to never stop doing what they love and most importantly never be scared to chase their dreams, while they were growing up, somewhere I forgot about this and they told me, "Practice what you preach!" I was teaching them life lessons but I was forgetting to apply them in my life. A small thing that happened last new year's, we had planned to go out to celebrate but something happened and we cancelled last minute. We still partied at home, we ordered food in and just before midnight, I pulled them to dance and simply jump around if nothing else. They did do as I told them to, because I'm the mom...but later on they reminded me that dancing makes me happy and they ensured I joined a dance class.

These little things they do sometimes makes me wonder who is the kid here? They look like kids but are much wiser than me (something I will never say in front of them!) whereas I look older but I guess not as wise!! With everything that we have gone thru together, I can actually say; the three of us have grown up together in our own ways and there have been times when as a single mother I have gotten over-whelmed and cried my eyes out, but at the end of the day when they hug me, I know that's all I need!

As they are growing up, we have learnt that the three of us need our own time and space. While coping with this has not been very easy for me, I ensure I respect their time and space and give them a breather. Doing this has made them more open with me and they tell me each and every detail of their lives and that includes their crushes and problems too.

My motherhood journey will continue for a long time and I will learn new things from my 'Teen-parents' (that's what I call them to ensure they do not grow up too soon and keep that child in them alive always!), I also know this I will always need my kids and I will always question who is the kid here??

CHAPTER TWENTY-ONE

All the single badass moms!

Free time? What is that?? I'm sure many of the single mothers out there would agree when I say this....Free time seems like a dream or a luxury! Why I chose to write on this topic? Lately I've been reading all these articles that have been showing only the tough parts of being a single parent and frankly speaking...these articles made me depressed. Yes I agree being a single parent is tough, but it is not a taboo and definitely not something to be ashamed of.

I am a single parent and even though I didn't choose to be one, the fact is I am and no this write up is not about how tough my life is and definitely not to show me as a victim of fate!

6 years of being a single parent has had its ups and downs but it has taught me an awesome lot. It has taught me an important lesson, my kids will never be happy if I'm not happy and I for one, am not a woman who would sit and cry over what happened and question everything that life throws towards me.

Like every other badass woman, I too am not the typical Mother who would sacrifice everything for her kids! Now don't get me wrong...I love my kids but that doesn't mean I put my life on hold for them. The initial years I had made this mistake, I would feel sorry for them since they had just one parent and in that I would end up fulfilling only their needs and ignore my needs. I used to feel guilty and would try compensating in every way possible, there was a time I wasn't working and I would still go and buy them what they demanded, not thinking how I am damaging them and myself in the process.

When I realised things were going out of hand and that maybe they would use this as an excuse to get things done their way, I sat down and made them understand.

Why am I saying all this? Well, just because like me there are several other women who are single mothers and they too may be giving into their kids' whims and fancies out of guilt. Maybe my experience may help them just a little. To all those women....let's rephrase or redefine single mothers. We are Single and we are Mothers, I suppose some of the lucky few who enjoy both the sides...we can act as whimsical as we want to, because we are single and ladies we are independent, smart, responsible (cause let's face it...we are mothers!), intelligent, sexy and hot! Who wouldn't be jealous of us...enjoying both the worlds!

So please live your life, because IT IS YOURS, NOBODY ELSE'S! Take care of your kids but at the same time make them independent and responsible beings who know that you are not just a mother, you have your own individuality too. They should know that you also have your own likes and dislikes especially when it comes to small things like food, tv channels and music. Also, while you treat them as equals and are open with them; they should know that no matter what happens they can never disrespect you, because you will not let them!

My kids know that no one can or will ever replace their father and they don't even need one, but they also know that if I like a guy and am in a relation, they don't need to fear it. Between the three of us, we never hide anything, no matter what is bothering any of us, we discuss it openly. They tell me about their crushes and I tell them about mine!

I agree it is not a smooth road, but it is a fun road. I follow one mantra in life which is very common, "look at the bright side" so when I feel absolutely low or have loads of stress about what the future holds and how will I cope with it all and will I be able to cope with it? All I do is think of all the good things and people in my life and it actually works!

So to all the single ladies, wear that lipstick and get your A-game on!

CHAPTER TWENTY-TWO

Go Goa, Gone!

So this happened yesterday, my son comes to me and tells me that he and my daughter are planning to go off to Goa for a vacation!

Yes! That happened!!

Back story:

I am a mother to two teenagers...trust me it's not as simple as it sounds. We have our ups and downs, but try our best to find the middle way that three of us are comfortable with!

Anyways, so coming back to the topic; its 2:30PM in the afternoon, I'm sitting and finishing this important mail I had to send and my son tells me about their plans of Goa. Now I was so involved in my work that I just said 'Okay' and the topic was over. The next few days there was no talk about this "trip" and I even forgot all about it.

One night just before sleeping, these kids come and ask me where their swim suits were kept and I very casually asked them where were they going for a swim that they wanted their costumes? That's when they realised that something was fishy! Okay, so usually we call for a 'family meeting' when important things are to be discussed. Next morning my son called a 'family meeting' in the hall and very seriously reminded me that he had specifically told me about going to Goa. He even gave me the specifics of what I was doing, where I was sitting when he told me and that I had said "Okay".

As a mother I was a little sceptical about their travelling alone, especially due to the Covid situation. I was restless and not because they were going to Goa, I knew they would be safe there since they were visiting their Aunt there; I was restless because they were to travel alone, I wouldn't be there. Thoughts kept me awake at night that I wouldn't be there with them, they were still my babies and what if they needed any protection, who would protect them? Not that I am good with kung-fu or I can karate-chop anyone who is attacking the kids..but I can certainly break that person's nose! Yes, I overthink situations that aren't there, but that's just how I am!

Next few days they behaved like angels, I was myself shocked to see this transformation....rooms tidy, clothes folded and STUDYING too! Cherry on the cake was that they ate whatever I cooked, without complaining even once! While I knew it was a trap being set for me to say "Yes" for the trip; seeing them behave the way they were, I was relaxed that they would not be lost on how to fold clothes and pack their stuff....they were responsible! I even gave myself a pat on the back for doing a good job in raising them to be responsible.

So the following evening, they made me pancakes with maple syrup and strawberries and sat with their "puppy dog eyes" staring at me while I ate my treat! Even though I had already made up my mind, still I waited till I finished my dessert and got ready for bed, I finally gave in to their wishes and said a YES! My babies were overjoyed and they gave me a big tight hug!

Their tickets were booked and their excitement was over the roof! These two were going on a solo trip (Yes their aunt is in Goa and yes they were going to be safe, but these two know how to manipulate their aunt into doing things they like; and yes she loves them a lot to let them manipulate her!) and here I was supposed to slog while they partied! But secretly I was glad they were going, less of work for me and they needed that break, WE needed a break from each other!

As they left for their trip, I couldn't stop myself from remembering the first time I took them to Goa, they were so little (not even 10!) and they were scared of sharks coming and eating them, that I would literally have to pretend to shoo away the fish for 5-10 minutes and that is when they would finally enter the water! Now they are all grown up, not scared of the water or fish and they certainly don't need me there to shoo away the fish...they say "we will catch the fish and cook it...Fresh from the water!"

This episode has taught me that just like the kids are confident about handling themselves, we as parents need to trust their instincts and just go with the flow. At the most they would not be able to be as responsible as they thought, but at least they tried....that's what matters at the end of the day. Instead of showing them their failure, we need to show them their strength, we need to support them. Our kids do support and comfort us when we are low, why can't we do the same?

CHAPTER TWENTY-THREE

Daddy's Smile Says It All...

I read a lot of blogs/write-ups on fathers and to be honest I envy everyone whether a girl or a boy who has or has had a father. Why you ask? Well, that's because I don't remember my time with my father!

I have spent only 8 years of my life with my Dad and frankly speaking I don't remember much from that time. What I do remember is his smile....my dad had the sweetest and the most reassuring smile ever!

I long to see his smile, I know there was so much love in his smile, he lit up our lives with all the time spent with us. Whenever I missed him, I remembered his smile...it said everything I needed to hear. While in school, whenever I had a fight, my Daddy's smile would calm me down.

When in college I had my first heartbreak, I remember all I needed was my daddy's smile telling me that this is just the first of many more heartbreaks till I find the one!

When I met my husband, I remember it was my Daddy's smile that I longed for and even though it came a little late, but I found his smile; and I knew no matter what he is always there for me.

When I had my first child, I needed his smile and I remember I have never seen him happier than that! My Daddy's smile was the broadest and full of pride to have a grandchild!

When tragedy struck and I was lost, it was my Daddy's smile that assured me everything was going to be alright!

When I started my life again, I required only my Daddy's smile to tell me to stop behaving like a victim of fate and be strong!

There are a lot of things my Daddy's smile says but the most important one is to never give up! I don't know what my father's smile would say and I don't need to because I have my Daddy in my Mommy!

I will always miss my father, but I know he left me a mother strong enough to be a father!

CHAPTER TWENTY-FOUR

Could You Love Yourself More...Please?

I read somewhere that being a parent means loving your children more than you've ever loved yourself.

My question is why do we have to love them more than ourselves? If I keep myself a priority, does that make me a bad parent? Actually, NO IT DOESN'T!

I am a great parent who loves her children to the moon and back, but I love myself more and that is what I am teaching my kids too. I don't want them to grow up and blindly follow a set of rules that have been going on for ages without question or reasoning.

There was a time I had a similar thinking, I had taken it for granted that my mother has to love me more than she loves herself and in the same way her mother loves her and when I have kids I would love them in the same way...more than myself!

But as I grew older I observed how my grandmother and my mother would not bother about their health but ensured all their kids were healthy. When I had my kids I too did similar stuff. I remember this particular incident when my son was 3 years old and my daughter was 2years, I had a ligament tear on my right leg. The doctor had specifically asked me not to move around and take rest, but me being a mother; I refused to take any help from my family and did everything I could for my kids. This was because I loved them, but it was more because I had the same thought process. I thought if I didn't do what they wanted, that would make me a bad mother!

Well, almost 11 years later, my right leg still hurts because I didn't give myself the rest I needed and I still become a 'bad mother' when I scold them....but now I don't care!

You see I have a very simple rule in life, "if I am unhappy how can I make anyone else happy?" It is the same thing that the cabin crew tells you before the plane takes off, "In the event of a decompression, an oxygen mask will automatically appear in front of you. If you are travelling with a child or someone who requires assistance, secure your mask on first, and then assist the other person." The same applies for parenting (whether the father or the mother)

Over the years this is one thing that I have learnt...learn to question everything that doesn't make sense to you. As a new parent, I did not and now 14 years into parenthood, me and my children make our own rules.

I do not compare my parenting style with anybody else and I ensure my kids also don't. I teach both my children to follow only those things that make sense when they become parents.

If only I had realised this early in life, I would have ensured my mother lives her life the way she wanted and not altered according to us. I wish I had the sense to ask her to re-marry and not slog the way she did to give us an amazing childhood. But what has happened cannot be changed, but I do not want the same applying to my children.

There are days I don't want to be a parent and that is absolutely okay, those are the days I don't want to even lift a finger. I let the children do everything, I make them responsible for running the house for the day and they love it. They learn new things, they learn their weaknesses (which we work on later), they learn how to manage money and most importantly they learn to be self-dependant and responsible humans.

So ladies, forget the old saying and love yourselves; because loving yourself more doesn't make you love your kids less.

CHAPTER TWENTY-FIVE

When my Lion cut his Mane!

There are many milestones in a person's life which when we reach, we learn how to cross and at the same time become wiser. For me, I still feel like I finished college like it was yesterday...but truth be told...I'm getting old!

When my kids were born again, I was there for their milestones and helped them get through them. Till now where my children are concerned 'milestones' meant celebrating their 10th birthday or the pre-teens, then there was them entering their Teens!

When my daughter entered puberty I knew what was to be done and she was prepared for it, but this time it was different...it was my son. He started asking me questions about the changes he was going through and I had no idea how to explain stuff to him!

Initially whenever he would ask a question, I would tell him "don't worry it's all normal, hormonal changes hai, it happens to everyone." I knew it was the dumbest reply since I wasn't convinced so I knew he wasn't. That's when I started reading about it all and sat with him and spoke with him about his body and what all changes he will be seeing.

I was finally done with that talk and when he turned 13, we were on our way back from a dinner (this is before the lockdown happened) and while waiting for the traffic signal to turn green, I noticed a long hair (mind you only 1 long hair) right below his chin and me being me...I just pulled it off! It didn't strike me that he was going to get more of them and then within a few weeks he started getting more hair...his beard started growing.

I knew immediately that this is going to be another milestone when he shaves for the first time. So I started consulting all the males in my family and finally it was concluded that till he turns 15 I wouldn't have to worry about it. I was relaxed!

I was wrong! on his 14th birthday his facial hair started looking too prominent, he has started to get a beard along with moustache on his face.

He had changed...from my little baby boy he was turning into a young man!

I searched google and got the same result saying it was too soon to shave! We decided to stick to the plan and wait till he was 15. I would like to add here that my son has curly hair just like me, so his head is full of thick curly hair which tend to be an issue in summers because it gets hot up there! Having said that, imagine a face with curly haired beard!!!!!

Every day I would ask him if the beard made him hot on his face and he would just get irritated with my constant questioning. Adding fuel to the fire was my daughter...she started teasing him by handing him a brush to comb his "mane" that's how the whole joke started. We teamed up and changed his name on our phone to 'lion', we teased him, questioned about his hair, till he would lose his cool.

Mean! I know I was being a bully, but that's how we are, I remember when my daughter waxed her hands and legs, he didn't take it too well. He kept on teasing her and irritating her because "her jungle was gone", but coming back to his beard, I would oil his hair and oil his beard too (just for fun) and I would tell him that he needs to oil it regularly!

A few days ago, finally we agreed to get his beard trimmed and thus began the task of finding the best trimmer for him. His grandfather and I spoke and concluded that initially we must buy a basic trimmer to let him get the hang of doing it on his own and finally his grandfather sent one all the way from Pune for him.

Our lion was finally trimming his mane. I shortened his beard using a scissor and used the trimmer to show him how to do it on one side. When I asked him to do it on his own, his hands trembled and he asked me to help him. I held on to his hand and helped him and in the middle of it I let go so that he could go on.

I'm so proud of this young man and it feels like yesterday when I first held his hands to make him take his first steps and later when he learnt how to cycle...these kids grow up too fast and there is nothing we can do except just be there and help them through all these milestones because they give us some very sweet memories which would last forever!

Oh yes I forgot to add my lion looks like a cub again after cutting his mane and yes I have been calling him a cub now! ;P

CHAPTER TWENTY-SIX

I am a Mother like no other

With Mother's Day around the corner, I teased my children by saying I would not be working that day and they will have to tend to all my whims and fancies for the day. Now the obedient children would say yes...but I have monsters and the reply I got was "we tend to your whims and fancies every day!"

No, they are not disrespectful, they love me and that's just how we roll! I was 23 years old when I had my son and I knew zilch about parenting, I was given loads of advice and loads of instructions about parenting.

My grandmother (mother's side) would get furious with me when I carried my son in a baby carrier, her exact words were, "I didn't know you are a monkey to carry your baby like one! He isn't too heavy that you keep him hanging on like this." She said it in a loving way because she couldn't stand anyone mishandling her great grandson. She knew I would get cheesed off that's why she would say it more and in mewari, so the word for monkey would be "baandriyo" and I would laugh.

My mother had a very different style of raising me and my sister and somehow I turned out to be an "outlaw" in the family. So like I mentioned I was 23 when my son was born...in fact I turned 23 exactly 18 days after he was born, so basically we grew up together. Later (only a year later) my daughter was born and we became the inseparable trio!

My experiences with the kids made me realise that there is no set pattern to raise your kids. What may work for one person may not work for another so I happily threw all the parental advices and books aside and trusted my instincts (which sometimes I feel get lost).

I come across a lot of mothers who ask me how did I explain my daughter about all the changes that happen in our body, how I explained my son about the changes he would be having etc., like I said I grew up with them so when my son was around 3 years and my daughter was also born. There would be days when I would have cramps and he would wonder why I am in pain, so for me it was easy to explain telling him the process and him seeing me buying pads was normal. Many family members got angry because of the way I handled this and I didn't care because had I not done it then...he would not have understood and taken care of his sister when she started her periods for the first time.

I still remember the first time we went to Sula fest together; the kids were 9 yrs and 10 yrs old and I got judgy/cold stares from random people because I had kids with me and it was like "What in the hell was she thinking to get her kids to such a place!!" believe me I could hear it even though they didn't say it. But what the heck! We had a blast and enjoyed till our legs hurt....these guys still tell their friends the stories of all the Sula fest and Octobrews they have gone for and their friends wonder when would they go!

I don't do all this to be in their good books or to prove anything to anyone. I parent them my way because for me it is better that they experience they want with me and in front of me so that they know that they have me always to guide them and help them to understand the difference between right and wrong.

There are days I am their mother, some days I am their father and then at times I'm a friend, they let me know whom they want me to be for that day and we do it...but every day, every single day I am ME and I do ME.

So please, don't let anyone teach you how to raise your kids. It is always a trial-and-error method for all parents and that changes with every phase of the child. What may work for you in dealing with your child may not work when he/she is a teen; what works for your 13-16yr old teen may not work when he/she is 17-19yrs; and so on. So please just be flexible and find a way that works for both you and your kids!

I have a fixed mantra that I follow, I do things my way, so next time if you try educating me about how I should be raising my kids; please know this that I am a nice person so I will respect what you say and hear you out; but ultimately, I will do what I want and the way I want!

Tales of a Limping Mom!

Lately life has been too perfect for me...with my kids behaving, getting good grades, work front being amazing (touchwood!), exercising on point (to the extent of old clothes fitting!) and me being in a happy place!

In the words of Marilyn Manson, "If things are too perfect, people are always so afraid that it's going to change, so they ruin it themselves." Well, it so happened with me too...I ruined my streak of perfection!

Now, for those who don't know me...I'm a badass mom to two teenagers. Why 'badass', because my children are badass and I'm keeping up with the BADASSIANS! ;p

Okay, that was a poor joke! But yes, it just so happened that while relaxing one fine afternoon and being grateful for everything and everyone, I asked my kids for a glass of water. Now, confession time, I was just feeling lazy to get up and my kids asked me to wait only for five minutes...BAS!!!

Now a normal person would be okay in waiting, but me being me...I jumped out of the bed to drink that water and ended up twisting my little toe! OUCH!! I yelled in pain and couldn't move all the toes in my left foot and it hurt really bad. I'm sure most of you must have experienced hurting the toes by side tables or corners, but this was twisted!

For the next 2-3 days I couldn't wear slippers, shoes or even walk barefoot. My foot was swollen and it hurt like hell. So, like any sane person I gave my foot rest. The next entire week my friend helped in getting us milk daily, the kids helped around the house and the maid bought the vegetables.

But for how long could I let this go on?

The problem was not with their helping, it was more about me becoming a liability. My kids were asking their friends to submit their school work because I couldn't drive, they were cancelling going to birthday parties because I couldn't take them and to top it all, they didn't complain!

That was it! Took matters in my own hands and started doing things around the house again. Skipping to 4 weeks later, my leg was still hurting but there wasn't any swelling. Now I was a bit concerned since I could no longer exercise, so I decided to show it to the doctor. It was a hairline fracture!

Now, usually when you have a fracture, one should get it plastered. I chose not to. Why!? You ask??? Well, my doctor tried convincing me to get my leg plastered but the only problem is that I would have been dependent on everyone again!

Being a single mom can be taxing at times and I agree that I have people around me who will help me no matter what the situation is....but this decision was mine!

The next 2-3 days I tied my leg using a crape bandage and as per the doctor's strict orders, rested with my leg elevated. The kids handled the house amazingly well but that lasted for only 3 days.. I was up and about limping but finishing the house chores and driving.

The troublesome duo was good enough to cheer me up, help me and being understanding. So, in return I started a new tradition in our house...movie nights with dinner and drinks of their choice on Saturdays. Well, we can have it any night, but we chose Saturday only to end the week on a nice and melodious note.

Life goes on and we have to keep moving along with it. The following weeks were more hilarious as we kept on trying to adjust to this limping situation. They would threaten me into resting and I would not listen, I drove them to get milk and other stuff required, they would shop. The kids would use my limping as an excuse to get out of meeting friends when needed and other times would try to pick me up just to know how strong they are.

My doctor is sweet enough to keep a check on me and he still gets mad at me for not resting and I still give him the same excuse that if I rest who will work! But he knows it as well as me, that the only excuse for not plastering my leg is that I hate being dependent and even though I know that my children are big enough to handle everything including me....I won't let them do it for long.

The limping has turned the tables at my place...here the kids have become the parents and I have become a kid high on sugar...a kid who cannot walk properly but has to run around the house doing stuff and not sit in one place.

Why I wrote about this? Well, it is not to have people pity me for being a single parent, but to know that it is okay. Three is never a crowd, we have our ups and downs, we learn things together but I know at the end of the day, my kids are growing up into amazing humans.

I have come across many people who have judged me only for being a single parent. People pity my kids for not having a father, but Hey! they have me and they don't need a father because we are enough. I wouldn't lie, there are times when I'm not okay being the only adult in the house, and I wish I had someone who could help me out. But then my kids prove every time that we are happy being the fabulous trio that we are and I know there isn't any place for a fourth person now.

Whether I'm limping or not I know that these two are and will always be my constants and all our experiences together bring us closer.

CHAPTER TWENTY-EIGHT

Sixteen, Seventeen or Forty? –Confused!

I am 16, going on 17....oh wait! Sorry, my bad....I am turning 40 in a couple of years...gone are the days of being 16 or even 20 for that matter! So, why am I singing this song since the morning? Oh yes! My son is turning 16 in a month and I can't keep calm!

For those who don't know me...I am a single mother to two children (one year apart) and I usually write about our lives... and my experiences of motherhood!

Lately, I feel a little left out and like I am missing out on a lot of stuff happening around me...I think it is called FOMO. Please excuse my slang! Yes, as I was saying....this feeling has somehow crept into me, believe me when I say....I have never been like this, people who know me; know that I HAVE BEEN THE PARTY ALL MY LIFE. So why now?

While I am a mother who dotes on her children and at the same time like all the mothers in this world...need some space away from them too; I also sometimes want to feel wanted again. They have become too independent for my liking!! I remember writing about this in an old blog of mine...17 again!

Being almost 16...he has his share of mood swings, he and I still don't agree on a lot of things, and most importantly, despite all of that, we try to find common ground!

No, this blog is not about how scary it is to have teenagers and how hard it is to handle them...this blog is about how I as a mother of two teenagers am trying to keep my sanity.

They say it takes a village to raise a child, I totally agree. So imagine having two villages to raise two children! While I do have the guidance and help from family, it does have its share of advices that I do not follow! I strongly believe that nobody can teach a person how to raise their kids. What applies to me and my kids might not be helpful to anyone else.

I see a lot of vlogs and reels on how to TEACH your kids manners, how to TEACH your kids to be good humans, respect elders and help the needy. Well, all my years of being a mother, I know one thing for sure...children follow what they see. So, please stop protecting the children from harsh realities and make them weak....let them learn their own lessons...this is how they would be strong and ready to face the world! If the parents follow something the kids automatically do the same. The basic rule of being organized and disciplined is to make your bed when you wake up. This is something that I have been doing since I was 7yrs old and when my kids were around the same age I made them do it too.

Dealing with kids who are almost 15 and 16, I still don't make a big hullabaloo about it. My son's farewell is around the corner, buying him clothes for that has been challenging to both my daughter and me! Why!? That is because he is soooooo very confused about what he wants to wear. Sometimes it's a white linen suit and sometimes it just another colour! To top it all when I advised him, he made fun of how old school my choice is!! The audacity I tell you! My blood boiled and my face was red with anger...I felt like holding him by his shoulders and shaking him hard, has he forgotten that I have been shopping for him even before he was born and he loved what I bought for him!!!! But nonetheless, I managed to keep my cool and sanity by taking him to the shop and making him try all the colours he wants....he gets irritated and I have a laugh. Next time he would think twice before commenting on my taste! The bugger's sense of style is because of me!!

But all said and done...I love my kids, we have a special bond! I used to laugh at people who said that parenting teenagers can be a very lonely time! Well now I am facing it.... With my son almost 16, he has his own friend circle with their own party plans, and with the New Year approaching, they are already planning a party! My daughter, on the other hand, has time, but she is a teenager, and she and her friends have plans...now I am free to plan something of my own! This is not what I want!

Yes you read it right! I don't want to plan anything that will leave these two ducklings out! I'd like to throw a party where both of them will be present and I can complain about how much I need a break from them! It cannot be the other way around!!! But it's not just the party; it's ME!

I have friends of all ages; the ones my age have young children, making it easier for them to travel, and the older ones have settled children, allowing them to travel... Except for me, no one else has children sitting for their boards this year!

The FOMO sadly is not due to my kids but all of my friends since they are travelling and have plans, whereas I have no plans because we have exams coming up! Now, I know that most of you will comment while reading that when my kids plan their own parties, I can also go out! That's the problem...all of the people and places I want to go are out of town!

Am I turning into one of those mothers who is afraid of the nest emptying!? Hell no! I can't wait for these kids to get into college and then move on with their lives and careers so that I am free!

I've spent most of my years being a mother and I know I will be a mother till my last breath, but there are times I need my space too! But like they say...this too shall pass! Just as I have boards this year and next year and the year after that (my kids are just a year apart); my friends will have their kids sitting for boards too someday and that my friend is the day I will have the last laugh! I will be partying like I'm 17 again!!!

CHAPTER TWENTY-NINE

Embracing Imperfect Motherhood: A Message to All Moms

To the mom, who feels invisible in motherhood...I see you

Do you ever feel like you're invisible in motherhood? Like your efforts and sacrifices go unnoticed, and no one really sees you for who you are?

I want you to know that I see you. Yes, you - the one reading this right now. You are loved, and your role as a mother is important beyond measure.

I know what it's like to question yourself and your decisions, to feel overwhelmed and exhausted, and to wonder if anyone really cares. But let me tell you, you are seen and heard. You are making a difference in your children's lives, and you are appreciated.

To the mom, who feels invisible in motherhood...I see you

Do you think that all the other mothers have it right? Your mother had it all figured out? Well, nobody is perfect and nobody can ever be perfect. Everyone screws up every now and then and THAT is perfectly fine. Mistakes teach us!

I didn't know anything about motherhood, I still make mistakes and I'm okay with it. I am happy being a perfectly imperfect mother!

To the mom, who feels invisible in motherhood...I see you

Cheer up! You are better than what you were yesterday. I know how overwhelming it is when the baby cries the whole day and nobody helps out. It's okay! being a mom is not easy, but it sure is not as difficult as everybody says.

You make a difference to that child's life. You are and will always be that child's first love and a person who can never be replaced!

To the mom, who feels invisible in motherhood...I see you

People are going to judge you, no matter what you do. Whether or not you go by the book, will not stop them from judging you as a mother. So, do whatever suits you and your child. Do what makes you happy, do what you feel is right for your child.

I still get judged over my parenting style and my kids are teenagers now! The only mantra to sail thru is to shut out everyone and only listen to your gut feeling. It may be wrong at times, but you will never know till you don't trust it!

To the mom, who feels invisible in motherhood...I see you

There will be times when you will feel like it was a mistake, you are not cut out to be a mother; times when you will want to run away leaving everything behind! It is okay and it is very natural to feel like this.

Don't feel too bad, I too feel the same most of the times and that is when I take out some "Me-time" without kids. Go for a movie or coffee or just a drive.

To the mom, who feels invisible in motherhood...I see you

Yes you are a Mother, but you are also a WOMAN. Don't kill that woman in you, don't forget that she exists too. While being a mother, give yourself a break from all and pamper the woman in you!

So the next time you feel invisible or unappreciated, remember that you are not alone. Reach out to a friend or a community of other moms who understand what you're going through; and know that you are loved and valued, just the way you are.

www.ingramcontent.com/pod-product-compliance
Lightning Source LLC
Chambersburg PA
CBHW032002140726
47988CB00019B/3145